SLAVERY
IN AMERICA

The Transatlantic
Slave Trade

By Duchess Harris, JD, PhD
with Marcia Amidon Lusted

Essential Library

An Imprint of Abdo Publishing | abdobooks.com

ABDOBOOKS.COM

Published by Abdo Publishing, a division of ABDO, PO Box 398166, Minneapolis,
Minnesota 55439. Copyright © 2020 by Abdo Consulting Group, Inc. International
copyrights reserved in all countries. No part of this book may be reproduced in any form
without written permission from the publisher. Essential Library™ is a trademark and
logo of Abdo Publishing.

Printed in the United States of America, North Mankato, Minnesota.
032019
092019

**THIS BOOK CONTAINS
RECYCLED MATERIALS**

Cover Photo: Morphart Creation/Shutterstock Images
Interior Photos: Everett Historical/Shutterstock Images, 4–5, 28–29, 44, 57, 77; World
History Archive/Newscom, 9; North Wind Picture Archive, 11, 65, 84; Shutterstock
Images, 16–17, 33; Sabena Jane Blackbird/Alamy, 23; Universal History Archive/
Universal Images Group/Getty Images, 24; SCFotos/Stuart Crump Photography/
Alamy, 26; Hulton Archive/Getty Images, 31; iStockphoto, 36, 38–39, 53, 61, 80;
Illustrated London News Ltd/Pantheon 10005138/SuperStock, 42; Red Line Editorial,
49; Max Milligan/AWL Images/Getty Images, 50–51; Splash News/Newscom, 62–63;
MPI/Archive Photos/Getty Images, 67; Ritu Manoj Jethani/Shutterstock Images, 71;
akg-images/Newscom, 74–75; Leemage/UIG Universal Images Group/Newscom, 83;
picturelibrary/Alamy, 86–87; AP Images, 89, 93; M. Stan Reaves/Alamy, 96

Editor: Alyssa Krekelberg
Series Designer: Laura Graphenteen

LIBRARY OF CONGRESS CONTROL NUMBER: 2018966007

PUBLISHER'S CATALOGING-IN-PUBLICATION DATA

Names: Harris, Duchess; Lusted, Marcia Amidon, authors.
Title: The Transatlantic slave trade / by Duchess Harris, and Marcia Amidon Lusted
Description: Minneapolis, Minnesota: Abdo Publishing, 2020 | Series: Slavery in
    America | Includes online resources and index.
Identifiers: ISBN 9781532119279 (lib. bdg.) | ISBN 9781532173455 (ebook)
Subjects: LCSH: Slavery--United States--History--Juvenile literature. | Slave trade--
    History--Juvenile literature. | Trafficking in human beings--Juvenile literature. |
    Africa--Juvenile literature.
Classification: DDC 382.4409--dc23

CONTENTS

SHIP OF GRIEF

I n the spring of 1829, Reverend Robert Walsh boarded a captured slave ship off the African coast. The ship held hundreds of enslaved people. As Rev. Walsh looked on, the hatchways were opened on the deck to reveal spaces barely three feet (0.9 m) high, packed with men and women captured in Africa.[1] The spaces were so small that people were forced to sit between each other's legs. They couldn't lie down or move around. They were all branded on the breast or arm with a mark, burned on with a red-hot iron, showing that they were now considered someone's property. The people were thin and weak, and many were sick. Children, lying next to the ship's walls, were barely conscious and couldn't stand or walk. Some of the enslaved people were chained together, and it wasn't unusual for a person to find

Slavers treated African captives as objects rather than as people.

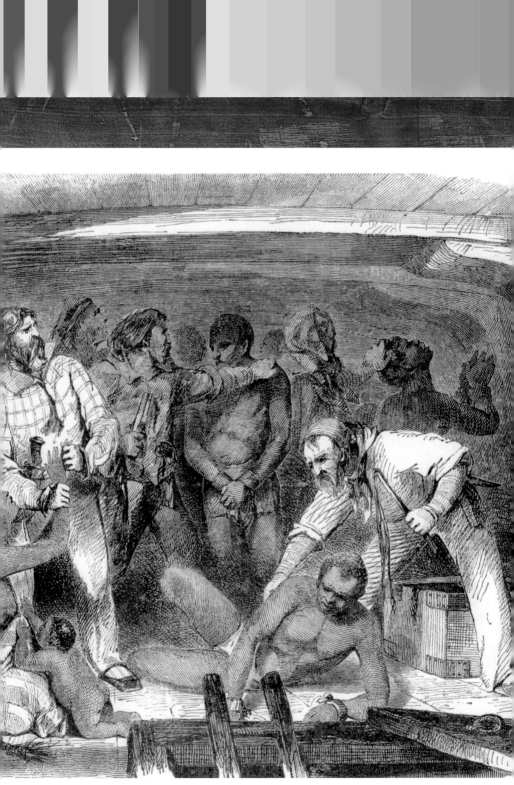

REV. WALSH'S VISIT

Rev. Walsh described his first visit to a slave ship in vivid details:

Our boat was now hoisted out, and I went on board with the officers. When we mounted her decks we found her full of slaves. . . . Over the hatchway stood a ferocious-looking fellow with a scourge [whip] of many twisted thongs in his hand, who was the slave driver of the ship, and whenever he heard the slightest noise below, he shook it over them and seemed eager to exercise it. I was quite pleased to take this hateful badge out of his hand, and I have kept it ever since as a horrid memorial of reality, should I ever be disposed to forget the scene I witnessed.[2]

himself or herself chained to a dead body.

These people had been captured from their homes in Africa and forced into slavery. They were packed onto slave ships, abused and beaten, and transported to the Americas to be sold to slaveholders. Many would die before they ever reached land.

Rev. Walsh's narrative of the slave ship was one of the most vivid descriptions of the slave trade. Another narrative, written by someone who experienced slavery firsthand, would become one of the first known eyewitness accounts of being enslaved. Some historians believe Olaudah Equiano was born in Africa around 1745, to the Ibo people who lived along the Niger River in the kingdom of Benin in West Africa. His people practiced agriculture, and the women spun and wove cloth. They had their own houses on small squares of land surrounded by red mud walls. Equiano was born the youngest son in a family of seven children. His father was a chief, an elder, and a judge in their village, and it was expected that Equiano would be the same when he grew up.

Slavery was a part of the Ibo culture, as it was with many African cultures, and Equiano's family owned slaves. But slavery among Africans wasn't the chattel slavery of Europe and the Americas, where slaves were treated as pieces of property. Slaves in Africa might be enslaved because they had to pay a debt or were being punished for a crime. Eventually, they might become part of their owner's family and be set free. However, the fear of being abducted to become someone else's slave was

THE DEBATE ABOUT EQUIANO

Historian Vincent Carretta says he found evidence that Olaudah Equiano wasn't born in Africa. Carretta notes that he discovered Equiano's baptism record, which lists his birthplace as Carolina, and a ship's list saying that Equiano was born in South Carolina. Carretta says that Equiano gathered stories from other slaves about leaving Africa for his autobiography. People argue that despite where Equiano might have been born, his autobiography is significant. Author David Dabydeen says, "What [Equiano] did was to take it upon himself to write the first substantial account of slavery from an African viewpoint but, as importantly, to write it with pulse and heartbeat, giving passion to the subject so as to arouse sympathy and support for the cause of abolition."[3]

always present, and when he was 11 years old, Equiano was kidnapped. Later, he wrote about his experience:

One day, when all our people were gone out to their works as usual, and only I and my dear sister were left to mind the house, two men and a woman got over our walls, and in a moment seized us both, and, without giving us time to cry out, or make resistance, they stopped our mouths, and ran off with us into the nearest wood.[4]

Equiano was separated from his sister. For the next six or seven months, he was taken from place to place and slaveholder to slaveholder, traveling farther and farther from his home. Eventually he arrived at the coast of Africa, where he was placed on a slave ship and had his first glimpse of white men. He was sold to the owner of a Dutch ship setting sail for the West Indies, which is a group of islands that separates the Atlantic Ocean from the Caribbean Sea.

The Passage to the Americas

Equiano's memoir of his time aboard a slave ship traveling from Africa to the Americas was monumental. It was the earliest widely read eyewitness narrative of an enslaved person captured in Africa and sent to another country. As an adult, Equiano was able to preserve a written record of

Olaudah Equiano worked to end slavery in Britain.

his life, giving historians a rare look into what he and other kidnapped Africans endured.

The voyage that Equiano took was just one leg of what's now called the transatlantic slave trade route, or the triangular trade route. In a very simplified form of the route, it resembles a triangle from Europe, to Africa, to the Americas, and back to Europe. The route carried goods, slaves, and agricultural products between these continents for four centuries. During this time, millions of Africans were taken captive and transported to other continents as slaves. The section of the route that went from Africa to the Americas, and which Equiano first traveled, is called the Middle Passage.

Equiano's description of traveling on a slave ship painted a grim picture of conditions endured by people who had been brutally taken from their homes and lives. Slaves were seen as property that could be sold for profit. Therefore, the ships carried as many captured people as possible, sometimes between 250 and 600 people.[5] This led to overcrowding. Equiano described his arrival on the ship:

> I was soon put down under the decks, and there I received such a salutation in my nostrils as I had never experienced in my life: so that, with the loathsomeness of the stench, and crying together, I became so sick and low that I was not able to eat, nor had I the least desire to taste any thing. I now wished for the last friend, death, to relieve me; but soon, to my grief, two of the white men offered me eatables; and, on my refusing to eat, one of them held me fast by the hands, and . . . tied my feet, while the other flogged me severely.[6]

Equiano goes on to describe the brutality of the white men on the ship, who often whipped enslaved people until they died. If a slave was particularly rebellious, the crew sometimes cut off the slave's hands, arms, or legs.

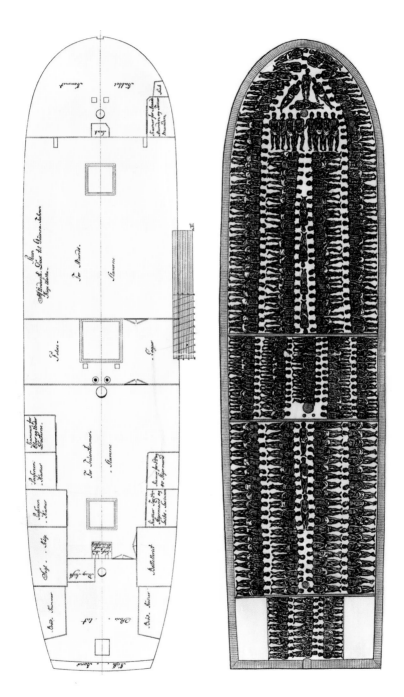

Captives were often packed tightly in slave ships.

Women, who were kept separately from men, were often sexually assaulted. The holds usually had buckets for urinating and defecating, although sometimes slaves had to relieve themselves over the side of the ship. However, since slaves were chained together, they often couldn't relieve themselves properly. Many became very sick. A British doctor who served aboard slave ships commented, "The excessive heat was not the only thing that rendered their

The *Henrietta Marie*

In 1700, off the coast of what is today Florida, a slave ship called the *Henrietta Marie* sank after hitting a reef. The wreck of the ship lay in the water for hundreds of years, until 1972 when treasure hunter Moe Molinar accidentally stumbled across a pile of iron shackles and realized he had found a slave ship. He took the ship's shackles and cannons and stored them in a warehouse in Key West, Florida. In 1983, a group of marine archaeologists became interested in Molinar's discovery. They visited the site of the shipwreck and discovered a bell with the name *Henrietta Marie*.

Research revealed that the ship began its voyage in London, England, then likely traveled to Gorée Island, just off the coast of Dakar in West Africa, and then to Port Royal, Jamaica, before it sank in hurricane winds near Florida. When the ship sank, there were no African captives on board—they had been delivered to Jamaica. It was the ship's captain and crew of slave traders who died, surrounded by the chains they had used on the enslaved Africans. In the early 1990s, the National Association of Black Scuba Divers placed a plaque on the *Henrietta Marie*, facing toward Africa, in memory of the enslaved Africans. The plaque reads: "In memory and recognition of the courage, pain and suffering of enslaved African people."[7]

situation intolerable. The deck, that is the floor of their rooms, was so covered with the blood and mucus which had proceeded from them in consequence of the flux [illness], that it resembled a slaughterhouse."[8]

Some slaves were so miserable that they stopped eating. Others jumped into the ocean and drowned, especially as they watched the coast of Africa receding and realized they would likely never see their homes again.

A Global World

Equiano survived the voyage and arrived in the British colony of Virginia in North America. His slaveholder was a lieutenant in the British Royal Navy, and his position enabled Equiano to travel and eventually receive an education in England.

Equiano's Story

As a slave, Equiano was sold several times. One of his slaveholders was a British Royal Navy officer, Lieutenant Michael Pascal, who renamed him Gustavus Vassa after a Swedish king. Equiano traveled with Pascal for eight years and learned how to read and write. Then he was sold to a London ship captain and later to a merchant named Robert King. Equiano worked as a deckhand, valet, and barber for King until he saved enough money from buying and selling crops on his own to purchase his freedom. Equiano spent 20 years traveling the world—even to Turkey and the Arctic—before returning to London in 1786. There he became a member of the Sons of Africa, a group of black men who campaigned for abolition. Equiano's autobiography of his capture and enslavement was published in 1789. It was one of the first books published by a black African writer.

Equiano became a successful businessman. He was also an outspoken abolitionist who worked to end the slave trade and resettle former slaves. He was just one of the millions of Africans who were taken from their homes, forced to live in the horrible conditions of the slave ships, and sold into what was often a lifetime of punishing work, physical and sexual abuse, poor living conditions, not enough food, and overall mistreatment.

The transatlantic slave trade was the first system of globalization, operating on an international scale and involving many countries. It involved nations and colonies on various continents and fostered new trade relationships, bringing a flow of goods, services, and slaves that produced profits for governments, companies, and individuals. However, this system had a steep, cruel price. It was built on the abuse and death of millions of people, and it also fostered what's still a continuing legacy of racism and inequality in the United States and other countries.

Equiano witnessed his first slave auction in Barbados, an island country in the Caribbean. Slave auctions were similar to livestock auctions, and the slaves were poked, prodded, and examined just like horses or cattle. They were then put on a platform, one at a time, and buyers would bid on them. The enslaved person was sold to the highest bidder. Often families, such as mothers and their young children, were split up and sold separately. Seeing a slave auction left Equiano deeply troubled about the treatment of slaves by white men:

> Is it not enough that we are torn from our country and friends to toil for your luxury and lust of gain? . . . Why are parents to lose their children, brothers their sisters, or husbands their wives? Surely this is a new refinement in cruelty, which . . . aggravates distress, and adds fresh horrors even to the wretchedness of slavery.[9]

How did a system that took advantage of millions of people begin? It took a combination of economics, geography, and technology to create the balance of factors that resulted in the transatlantic slave trade.

DISCUSSION STARTERS

- Why do you think so many people and countries supported the slave trade?

- Why do you think someone would want to be involved in the slave trade?

- What was so unusual about Olaudah Equiano in this time and place? Why is his voice important?

CHAPTER TWO

AFRICA BEFORE THE SLAVE TRADE

The slave trade lasted for four centuries, beginning in the middle of the 1400s. Before it began, Africa consisted of many thriving societies, although slavery wasn't unknown in Africa. Some European slave traders tried to justify their actions by claiming that Africa was a backward land and that Africans were inferior to Europeans. However, Africa had a long history of strong, technologically advanced societies long before North America was colonized in the 1600s, and even before Europeans developed sophisticated cultures and technology. In fact, Africa may have been home to the oldest state to exist anywhere

Ancient Egypt was one technologically advanced African society.

in the world. The ancient kingdom of Ta-Seti, located in what is now Nubia in Sudan, existed thousands of years ago. For much of ancient history, Africa was much more advanced than any other continent and reached high levels of political, scientific, and economic development.

One of the most famous African civilizations was that of the ancient Egyptians. Over thousands of years, the Egyptians developed a society that was advanced in areas such as mathematics, science, medicine, and technology. Even the ruins that still stand from Egyptian culture are impressive in their scope and engineering knowledge.

TA-SETI

Egypt was long considered the oldest civilization on Earth. But in 1962, a research team from the University of Chicago Oriental Institute discovered a civilization in Nubia that was older than Egypt. It included an area from northern Sudan to southern Egypt and was ruled by a dynasty of pharaohs. Some literature referred to the area as ancient Ethiopia. The Bible called it Kush. However, it's now called Ta-Seti. Archaeologists estimate that the first kings were ruling Ta-Seti in 5900 BCE.

Artifacts and structures from the site were discovered only because of a massive effort by archaeologists in the 1960s to rescue, record, and document as much as possible about the area before two dams were built nearby. The archaeologists found palaces, representations of the falcon god Heru, and the beginnings of a sacred writing system known as the Medu Neter—which the Greeks called hieroglyphs. Statues of ancient Ta-Seti pharaohs also wore the same distinctive crowns as the later Egyptian pharaohs.

The Egyptians used slaves for much of their workforce. However, slavery in Egypt wasn't like the system of slavery that developed in the Southern United States or other places in the world, where slaveholders completely owned and controlled the slaves. Egyptian slaves were often prisoners of war, criminals, or poor people who voluntarily sold themselves into servitude because of poverty or debt. They usually had a limited period of enslavement, which was more like indentured servitude. Indentured servants voluntarily sign an agreement to work as servants for a specified length of time and are then released, and their children are free people from birth. Most slaves worked as household servants, did administrative tasks, or worked in agriculture.

LANDS OF GOLD

The kingdom of Ghana—in what is now Mauritania, Mali, and Senegal in West Africa—was one of the wealthiest countries in the medieval world because of its trade in gold, ivory, and slaves. Ghana had many gold mines and established a thriving trading system with North Africa and Europe. The domestication of the camel as a pack animal also helped increase trade. Between 400 and 1100 CE, Ghana was an international crossroads, both economically and culturally. This part of Africa was known as the Gold Coast because of its gold. Arabic traders who

The Business of Slavery

Between the 600s and 1400s, Africa began to develop states and countries and became more sophisticated. During that time, inequality among citizens in those states increased. This inequality was especially apparent between the rich and the poor and between people who were free and those who were servants or slaves. Before that time, most slaves were treated like poor farmers rather than enslaved people. They could even own property. But as the practice of capturing and enslaving other tribes became a way to make money, slavery became part of states' trading relationships. And as the demand for slaves increased—first with Arab traders and eventually with European traders—the exploitation of poorer people also increased. A slave's status was no longer one of an indentured servant or punished criminal but rather an economic asset for the slaveholders. It was also an incentive to capture more slaves, since they could be sold for more money.

came to Ghana between 800 and 1000 CE wrote about the kingdom's wealth. One Arabic trader wrote, "Behind the king stand ten pages holding shields and swords decorated with gold, and on his right are the sons of the [vassal] kings wearing splendid garments and their hair plaited with gold."[1] Ghana's wealth also grew because it taxed goods coming into and leaving the country.

Benin was another early wealthy society in Africa. Around the 1300s, Benin was thriving. It had a strong standing army and a powerful ruler who expanded the country's territory and created a structured society where he owned all the land.

Benin craftsmen were known for their skill in creating figurines and masks from bronze, brass, ivory, and copper. They traded with Europeans, exchanging palm oil, ivory, cloth, pepper, and slaves for metals, salt, cloth, and guns. Benin was also a link between Europeans and tribes that lived in interior Africa. Benin served as an important part of the transatlantic slave trade, as it captured men, women, and children from rival tribes and sold them to slave traders from Portugal, France, and England.

The last great empire in Africa was Mali, which held power until the early 1600s. At its height, Mali spanned an area from the Atlantic coast to the central portion of the Sahara Desert. It was also rich in gold. Mali, like Ghana, also taxed all goods that came into and out of the country. While any gold nuggets mined belonged to the king, the people often used gold dust as a form of currency. Smaller kingdoms that belonged to Mali paid

GHANA'S SLAVE CASTLES

Between 1482 and 1786, Europeans built many castles and forts along Ghana's Atlantic coast. They were built to serve as protected trading posts for the gold trade, but eventually they became holding places for thousands of captured Africans awaiting transport to other parts of the world. These castles were the last memory most Africans would have of their homeland. The castles had a door opening onto the ocean called the door of no return. The captured Africans were lowered from the door into boats and taken to slave ships out at sea.

taxes using items such as arrows, rice, and lances. The
city of Timbuktu in Mali became a center for learning and
scientific study.

KINGDOMS AND SLAVERY

Slavery existed in many ancient cultures such as Greece,
Rome, and Egypt long before the beginning of the
transatlantic slave trade. Slavery did not originate in Africa,
but a form of slavery existed there.

As in many other African cultures, slavery existed
in Mali for centuries before Europeans began their
slave trade. However, it wasn't uniform, and different
regions practiced different forms of slavery. As with most
African societies, slaves fell into one of several categories.
Some were purchased or captured, while others were
born as slaves to enslaved parents in a household. Some
were prisoners of war. Slavery was an accepted part of
war—a way to supply a kingdom or country with needed
labor while subduing other tribes or kingdoms. Other
enslaved people were sentenced to slavery as punishment
for crimes. Still others were sold into slavery by their
poverty-stricken families.

A slave trade within Africa was established in
700 CE to supply Africans to the slave markets along the
Mediterranean Sea and then to the Middle East and Asia.
This route was known as the trans-Saharan trading route,

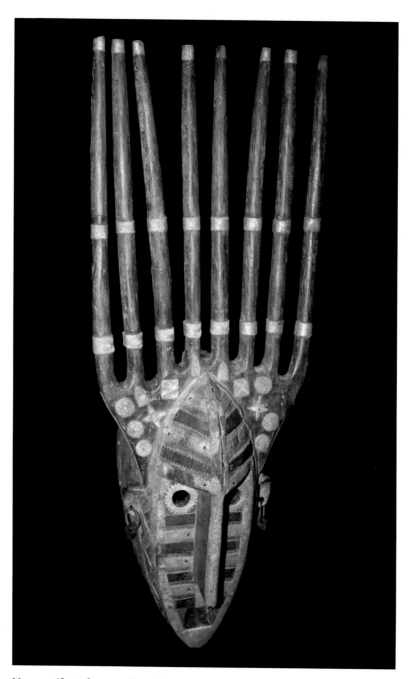

Many artifacts from ancient Africa, such as ceremonial masks, are displayed in museums. This mask is thought to be from Mali or Guinea.

Throughout the slave trade, Africans were sometimes chained or roped together after being captured.

because it crossed the Sahara Desert between Africa and the Mediterranean, continuing on to Europe. Because of this route, some enslaved Africans made their way to other parts of the world through trading of goods such as crops. As a system was already in place for trading enslaved African captives, this process eventually helped Europeans and North Americans capture and enslave many Africans for the transatlantic trade.

EUROPE AND AFRICA

The established trans-Saharan trading route wasn't only a way to trade goods such as gold, ivory, and salt. It was also the means for Europeans to access Africa. As early as the 700s, Muslim forces from North Africa, known as Moors, raided areas of what are today known as Spain and Portugal. They brought their culture, knowledge, and building and engineering technology with them. Many areas of Spain still show the influence of Islamic architecture. Spanish culture also has many Arabic influences, such as music, food, and art. The Muslim forces also brought the knowledge of their African trading routes, as well as tales of the vast supply of gold found there, which intrigued Portuguese explorers. Starting in the 1300s, these explorers began investigating the coast of Africa and making maps and charts of the area.

The stage was set for the transatlantic slave trade to

LOUIS ASA-ASA

Louis Asa-Asa was a slave captured in a raid on his African village when he was 12 or 13. The dates of his birth and death are unknown, but he is known to have been in London in 1826, where several abolitionists helped him write a narrative of his life. He describes how British goods were often used to purchase African captives: "[The captives] were sold for cloth or gunpowder, sometimes for salt or guns; sometimes they got four or five guns for a man: they were English guns, made like a master's that I clean for his shooting."[2]

The Mosque-Cathedral of Córdoba in Spain was built while the area was under Islamic rule.

take root. As Europeans established newer trading routes that reached farther around the world than ever before, creating new enterprises and technologies in the process, the need for labor was great. And with a system already in place for trafficking humans for enslavement, it was only a matter of time before the slave trade began to reach far beyond Africa's borders.

DISCUSSION STARTERS

- Why do you think that so many ancient cultures had slaves?
- What kinds of economic and social circumstances helped create slavery in certain countries?
- How did the establishment of trading routes change the world?

CHAPTER THREE

EUROPE STEPS IN

A frica had many sophisticated societies and developed its own trading systems and routes for both goods and enslaved humans. As these trade routes began to reach Spain and Portugal, word of Africa's riches began circulating through Europe. While the first Europeans who came to Africa were looking for gold, they eventually discovered not only a thriving slave trade between Africa and its neighbors but also the structure and population level to supply slaves to the rest of the world.

PORTUGAL AND AFRICA

Like many European traders during the 1400s, Portuguese traders hoped for a way to reach South Asia by ship. There, they could find valuable

Europeans would sometimes keep their captives in compounds before forcing them onto slave ships.

Prospect of the European Factorys, at Xavier or Sabee. from Marchais.

commodities such as gold, fabrics, and spices and bring them back to Europe to trade. It was this search for Asian riches that first spurred the Portuguese to sail down the coast of West Africa in 1444. They would bring the first African slaves from northern Mauritania to markets in Portugal.

Why was Portugal the first European country to investigate the coast of Africa? It had many advantages that led it to dominate sea travel and trading at that time. From 1346 to 1353, the black plague killed 60 percent of Europe's population, or about 50 million people.[1] But Portugal was geographically isolated enough to be protected from the spread of the disease. It was also able to pool its resources to fund expeditions. Portugal had a superior fleet of ships because of its contact with Islamic countries and knowledge, which had helped those countries establish lucrative trading networks of their own. This included much better knowledge of mathematics and sailing technology, such as the best shapes for ships' sails and hulls, as well as advanced weapons. These advantages allowed the Portuguese to become extremely successful in world trade in the 1400s and 1500s.

With those advantages, the Portuguese explored most of the West African coast by the 1600s. Travelers made maps of their explorations. The maps were valued for

By the 1400s, Lisbon, Portugal, was an important operational center for the country's exploration.

how well they transcribed Africa's complex coastline. The Portuguese developed a healthy trade in gold, ivory, and pepper.

EXPANDING AFRICA'S SLAVE TRADE

The Portuguese also found another commodity to export from Africa: slaves. The Portuguese kidnapped people from Africa's west coast, enslaved them, and took them back to Europe. In just their first 200 years of trade, the Portuguese took more than 175,000 enslaved people back to Europe and eventually to the Americas.[2] So many African slaves were taken to the Portuguese city of Lisbon that it's estimated that by the early 1500s, people of African descent made up 10 percent of its population.[3]

Some of the first places Europeans established international trade were the islands off Africa's western coast, including the Canary, Cape Verde, Madeira, and Azores Islands. Beginning in the 1300s, Europeans built trading posts and established sugarcane plantations on these islands. By the 1490s, sugar plantations were built on the island of São Tomé, off the West African coast.

Plantations were a new form of agriculture because they focused on growing crops for trading with others rather than feeding the farmer's family or community. This same plantation model was eventually used for crops such as tobacco, rice, cotton, and indigo, which is a type of plant used to make blue dye.

Sugar was in high demand in Europe after the Crusades, which were a series of religious wars between Christians and Muslims. During these wars, people of both religions wanted to gain control of lands they perceived as being holy. A total of eight major Crusade expeditions occurred between 1096 and 1291, bringing many Europeans to the Middle East and exposing them to civilizations and cultures they had never encountered before. These Europeans found sugar in the Middle East and brought it back home.

The Canary Islands can support the growth of many crops, such as bananas, oranges, coffee, sugarcane, tobacco, and grapes.

Before the Crusades, the only sweetener Europeans knew was honey. Sugar became a luxury, and it could also be used to make alcoholic beverages. Producing sugar was labor intensive. It took many workers to grow the sugarcane and process it into sugar. At first, the Europeans enslaved natives who lived on the coastal Canary, Cape Verde, Madeira, and Azores Islands, but soon they required more workers. They began bringing enslaved Africans to the islands.

TO THE AMERICAS

The Portuguese wouldn't maintain their advantage in the slave trade for long. Soon the Spanish were also involved in slave trading, kidnapping Africans from what is today Benin, Nigeria, and Cameroon. In 1518, they were the first to take enslaved Africans directly to the Americas. Before that, slaves were brought from Africa

SUGAR

How is sugarcane processed into sugar today? The process hasn't changed much since the era of sugar plantations that used slave labor, except the machinery is no longer powered by water or fire. Granulated sugar starts as sugarcane, a tall grass with long, thick stems that grows in tropical climates. Workers chop down the stems, leaving the roots intact so they will grow again the next season. The cut canes then go to processing plants where huge rollers crush them, extracting the cane juice. The juice is boiled until the water evaporates. The juice is boiled again until sugar crystals begin to form. Then a machine spins the liquid to separate the crystals from the remaining liquid, which is molasses. In this final stage, the raw sugar looks like brown sugar. It's refined into white sugar when it reaches the country where it will be used.

to Spain, packed onto slave ships there, and then taken to the Americas.

In 1545, after Spain had signed the Asiento agreements, which allowed other nations to transport Africans to Spanish colonies, most of the slave traders coming into Spanish and American ports were Portuguese. Approximately 240,000 enslaved Africans were taken to Spanish colonies in the Caribbean and Central America before 1641, but even more were taken to Brazilian ports, where most Portuguese traders were based.[4]

MORE COUNTRIES JOIN THE TRADE

Like the other Europeans, the Dutch quickly joined the slave trade. Between 1596 and 1829, Dutch traders transported roughly 500,000 enslaved Africans across the Atlantic Ocean to North America.[5] Many of its slave ships first stopped at the Caribbean islands of Curaçao and Saint Eustatius. Some slaves on these ships were carted back to Spain. Others were sold before the last part of the journey to other slave colonies or to the United States. The Dutch also shipped another 500,000 slaves to work on sugar plantations in Brazil.[6]

Britain would become one of the largest slave traders. When it entered the transatlantic slave trade in the 1600s, it quickly became larger and more powerful than all of the other European trading nations. British ports would end up outfitting one-third of all the transatlantic slave voyages made during the 1600s. Britain was also responsible for taking almost one million enslaved Africans to the island of Jamaica and 500,000 to Barbados.[7] Sugar was grown in both of these places. Slave trading and slave labor became an essential part of the enormous British system of trade and financing until Britain made slave trading illegal in 1807 and finally abolished slavery itself in 1834.

FRANCE AND THE CODE NOIR

France also played a part in the slave trade. By the 1700s, it was the third-largest country conducting slave trading, behind only Portugal and Britain. The enormous number of enslaved Africans that it transported—1.3 million—

Millions of Africans were sent to the Caribbean.

went to Guadeloupe and Martinique, but mostly to
Saint-Domingue, which is now Haiti.[8] These three
French-Caribbean colonies, which also produced sugar,
were bigger and more productive than the plantations
that Britain or Spain owned. French ships carried slaves
to Dutch Guiana and other Caribbean islands. They also
brought their human cargo to the Mississippi delta in the
United States in the late 1700s, including what would
eventually be Louisiana.

French slaves and their slaveholders in the French
Caribbean colonies, especially Haiti, were also forced to

follow the Code Noir. This series of rules regulated the relationships between slaveholders and slaves as well as the statuses of free blacks and slaves. King Louis XIV of France established the Code Noir in 1685, but it was revised in 1789 specifically to address the issue of slavery. The Code Noir would remain in effect in the French Caribbean until 1848. According to Nicole Atwill, a foreign law specialist, "The Code's sixty articles regulated the life, death, purchase, religion, and treatment of slaves by their masters in all French colonies."[9]

These major countries became involved in the slave trade because of the enormous opportunities for profit and business development. With these traders in place, a global ocean route that was the most advantageous to this new economy soon solidified: the transatlantic slave trade.

DISCUSSION STARTERS

- Why do you think so many European countries captured and enslaved people, particularly from Africa?

- How did sugar production and sugar plantations support the slave trade? Were there other crops that also supported the trade?

- If so many European countries hadn't stepped into the slave trade, do you think the trade would have expanded as much as it did? Explain your reasoning.

CHAPTER FOUR

TRANSATLANTIC TRADING

The expanding European colonies needed labor. The places that had established a profitable trade through enslaving Africans—Portugal, Spain, Britain, Holland, France, Sweden, Denmark, and North America—had that labor. Many of the new colonies Europeans established were unable to force native peoples to work for them for long periods of time. The native peoples weren't resistant to the diseases that Europeans brought with them, resulting in a high rate of fatalities. More than 90 percent of all indigenous peoples in the Americas are estimated to have died because of colonization.[1] Europeans also weren't accustomed to working in hot, tropical climates. So these colonies chose to force Africans into slave labor. Africans were used to tropical

Captives were forced to wear heavy shackles on board slave ships.

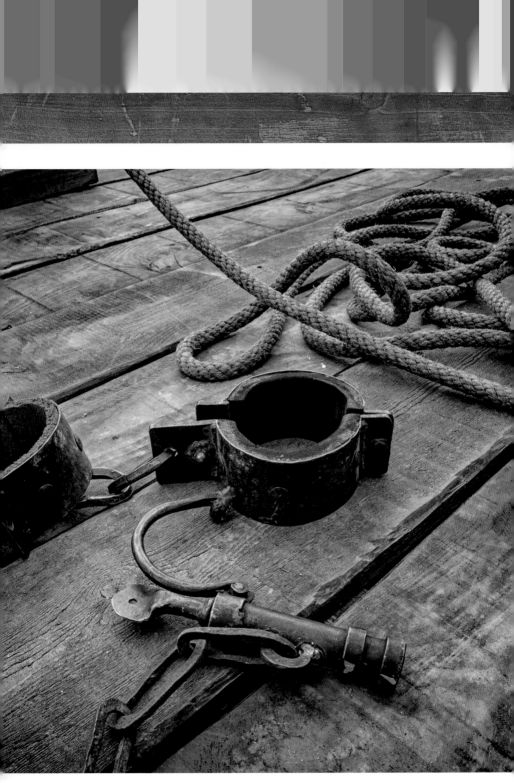

conditions, had a natural resistance to the tropical diseases, and often had experience growing crops and raising animals. Europeans took advantage of these things.

Many Africans were captured and enslaved by European expeditions that traveled in from the coast to find them. However, it wouldn't have been possible for slave traders to enter Africa and take captives without some involvement from African leaders. Some Africans were enslaved with the permission or full cooperation of African kings and merchants. In return, the African leaders received goods such as cowrie shells (which were a form of money), beads, brandy, guns, horses, and cloth. Even the forts that Europeans built on Africa's west coast were located on land that Africans either gave or leased to them. However, Africans received very little real economic value from trading with Europeans. The continent lost millions of its people. Many of its societies suffered as well, placing

CHANGING VIEWS

The Europeans who purchased and enslaved Africans treated them as objects, similar to furniture or domestic animals, with no human rights at all. Europeans also tried to get some of Africa's rulers to think in a similar way. They wanted the rulers to consider some of their fellow Africans as inferior, making it acceptable to sell them to European slave traders. Those traders used bribery and corruption to persuade elite Africans and African slave traders to go along with the European traders' ideas. That gave traders access to more Africans who could be enslaved.

Africa in an unequal relationship with Europe that later
helped Europeans conquer and colonize portions of Africa.

THE ROUTE

The interconnected economy of slaves, labor, and goods
transported across the Atlantic Ocean created a route
that's sometimes simplified as the triangular trade. This
term is based on the pattern created by the cycle of trade
between Europe, Africa, and the Americas. Each part
of the triangle was vital to the other two, as producing
goods required slave labor, transporting the slaves, and
transporting goods back to buyers in Europe. But the
pattern of exchange was a more complicated network
than a simple triangle. There was no single trade route.
For example, according to the Trans-Atlantic Slave Trade
Database—an authoritative source on slaving journeys—
almost 40 percent of captive Africans came to the
Americas on ships that sailed directly from Africa to the
Americas.[2] In these cases, the route was bilateral instead
of triangular.

However, in the simplified version of the route, the
first leg of the journey began in Europe, with ships loaded
with goods. When these ships arrived in Africa, the slave
traders exchanged the goods for captive slaves. Most of
the goods were guns and ammunition, desired by African
kings and merchants to help expand their territories

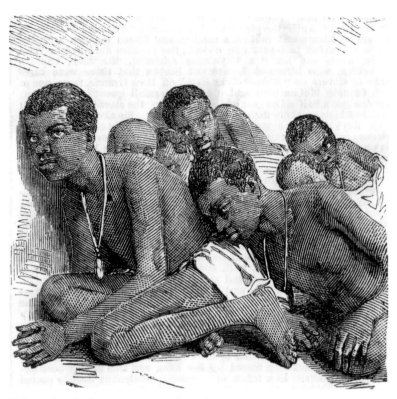

Africans faced inhumane, cramped conditions while en route to the Americas.

within Africa, but they could also include rum. The process of exchanging goods for enslaved captives could take anywhere from one week to several months.

The next leg of the transatlantic journey took place from Africa across the Atlantic Ocean to the Americas. Once the enslaved Africans reached the Americas, they were sold throughout the continent to supply labor for plantations and other enterprises. These enslaved laborers were then forced to produce high-demand goods such as tobacco, cotton, and sugar, which were then shipped back to Europe as the third leg of the triangle. Slave traders used some of the money made from selling these goods in Europe to purchase trade goods to take back to Africa and exchange for more slaves, which began the triangle process once again. The entire process of traveling the three legs of the triangle took about 18 months.

But historians note that it's important to recognize that the actual trade route was more complicated than this. Historian Sean Kelley says:

> Even when restricted to the British, French, and Dutch trades, the term "triangular trade" conveys the false impression that it was a closed system. In reality, the slave trade was a vast enterprise, assembling goods from across the globe, exporting and re-exporting them to Africa for captives who were then carried to the New World to labour at a variety of tasks. Geometry doesn't even begin to capture it. [3]

TECHNOLOGY MAKES IT POSSIBLE

Advancements in technology helped make the transatlantic slave trade possible. These developments occurred primarily during the 1700s, driven by the need for increased profits from slave trading. First of all, a fully rigged, efficient sailing ship was vital to transporting both

Enslaved people were forced to work the cotton gin.

slaves and goods. Adding rudders to the rear of the ship and using three masts for sails instead of one or two made it possible to sail down the coast of Africa and eventually across the Atlantic. Bigger ships were also needed in order to transport enough goods and captives to make the trip economically worthwhile. The steerage level, which is the lower passenger level in a ship's hull, was often eliminated, with the space converted to two decks instead.

The slave trade also relied on the manufacture of guns, which were essential for trading with the African kings and merchants who supplied captives for enslavement, or who at least gave their permission for slave traders to capture Africans. Guns, many of them manufactured in Britain, were imported into Africa in the second half of the 1700s.

Between the late 1700s and the abolishment of the British slave trade in 1807, British manufacturers went from being able to produce tens of thousands of guns a year to being able to produce millions. This was partly due to the advances in technology that enabled mass production of guns, but it was also because manufacturers were choosing gun designs that weren't necessarily the best firearms but could be mass produced most quickly.

Finally, technology such as the invention of the cotton gin, which made it easier to process cotton quickly for overseas shipment, also contributed to the growth of the transatlantic slave trade. More farmers grew cotton, creating a greater demand for slave labor and increasing the value of the traders' ships filled with human cargo. The invention of the cotton gin also strengthened the slave trade within the United States. It made cotton production easier, so people wanted additional slaves to do the work and expand production.

FINDING SLAVE LABOR

The success of the transatlantic trade depended on ripping Africans from their homeland and enslaving them in order to meet the increasing demand for slave labor. At first, many enslaved Africans were political captives, taken by one African tribe or group during war with another. Around 1735, Venture Smith, a six-year-old African prince, was captured by another tribe and sold to slave traders. He later recalled his first encounter with the slave traders: "The very first salute I had from them was a violent blow on the head with the fore part of a gun, and at the same time a grasp round the neck. I then had a rope put about my neck."[4] Venture was taken to the United States and became a slave in Rhode Island.

Trapped

Some Africans were entrapped by traders in their own villages. The Works Progress Administration (WPA) was a government agency during the Great Depression (1929–1939). The WPA employed millions of unemployed Americans for public works projects, including recording oral histories. One WPA project in the 1930s collected the narratives of former slaves whose ancestors had been taken from Africa. Many had a similar story to tell. John Brown, a former slave in Alabama, told the story of his grandmother's experiences when she was captured by slave hunters. She had explained how slave traders came to the coast and left "bright things and trinkets on the beach" for a couple of days.[5] The Africans would collect these things until they felt comfortable enough to approach the ship. Once the Africans were on the ship, the slave traders would set sail. Brown said once this happened:

Folks on the beach started to crying and shouting. The ones on the boat was wild with fear. Grandmother was one of them who got fooled, and she say the last thing seen of that place was the natives running up and down the beach waving their arms and shouting like they was mad. They boat men come up from below where they had been hiding and drive the slaves down in the bottom and keep them quiet with the whips and clubs.[6]

Slaves were sold in slave markets on the African west coast to traders from European countries. But political captives were a limited supply, and soon slave traders traveled into Africa to kidnap captives. Many of these Africans lived in small agricultural communities and had farming skills, making them even more desirable for plantation labor.

Whether they were bought from African slave markets, sold by African kings or tribes as political prisoners of war, or kidnapped by European slave traders, all enslaved Africans ended up in similar circumstances: awaiting shipment in the transatlantic trade. After being held for varying amounts of time in fortress-like structures on the African coast, they were forced onto slave ships. Some would survive the voyage to North America, and some would not.

DISCUSSION STARTERS

- Is the colonization of one country or area by another ever a good thing? Explain your answer.

- What do you think are the main factors that contributed to the transatlantic slave trade?

- How would you feel if you were taken away from your home and treated as human cargo?

THE TRANSATLANTIC TRADE ROUTE

Some historians call the transatlantic slave trade "a dramatic encounter of history and geography."[7] It was the first time that a global trade system emerged, linking various continents and countries in one commercial and economic enterprise. While most maps show a simplification of the three-legged trade route between Africa, Europe, and North America, the actual routes varied from the 1400s to 1800s. It's also possible to map the flow of African captives from different regions of their home countries to the Caribbean and South America. These maps show where the majority of enslaved people were taken from at different points during the 400 years of the slave trade.

Sugar, cotton, coffee, and tobacco

Weapons, cheap jewelry, etc.

Enslaved Africans

Zone of slave importation

BRITAIN

EUROPE

NORTH
AMERICA

NORTH
ATLANTIC
OCEAN

NORTH
PACIFIC
OCEAN

AFRICA

SOUTH
AMERICA

SOUTH
PACIFIC
OCEAN

SOUTH ATLANTIC OCEAN

CHAPTER FIVE

THE MIDDLE PASSAGE

S prinkled along the coast of Ghana are the remains of structures that are a reminder of the transatlantic slave trade and the Africans who were captured for enslavement. Known as slave factories, slave forts, trading houses, or slave castles, these buildings housed captured slaves until they were put onto ships for the Middle Passage to the Americas. They also served as trading posts and defensive structures for European slave traders, as well as symbols of prestige and power.

In these buildings, enslaved Africans were often kept in dungeons after the sudden and violent loss of their communities, cultures, and ways of life. Eventually they were taken to small boats that ferried them into deeper water, where they were

One slave fort on the Ghana coast is called Elmina Castle. It was built by the Portuguese in 1482.

loaded onto slave ships. Slave traders might buy captives from one fortress or castle, or travel up and down the African coast until they had reached their ship's capacity for slaves. Ten to 15 million enslaved captives would leave Africa this way, and two million of them died on the journey.[1]

SLAVE TRADE AND SHIPS

The voyage across the Atlantic Ocean was called the Middle Passage because it was the middle leg of the simplified three-part transatlantic trade route that began and ended in Europe. The captives had no idea where they were going or why, because no captured Africans ever returned to share their experiences. Some slaves were told that they would be working in fields on farms, but this was difficult for Africans to believe because farming, in their experience, didn't take a lot of time or require so many people.

Sailing across the Atlantic to North America could take eight weeks or longer. At first, traders adapted regular merchant sailing vessels to hold as few as 30 to as many as 700 slaves, depending on the size and design of the ship.[2] Later, ships were built specifically for carrying more slaves. The African captives were packed onto these ships. They had no choice except to sit or lie down where they were held, and they were so closely packed together that any

Plantation owners used many enslaved people to make money.

movement was difficult. There was very little ventilation, as the only light and air came in from wooden grates that opened onto the ship's deck, and it didn't reach very far. The smell of human waste filled the cramped area. The conditions made disease common, especially dysentery, adding vomit and other bodily fluids to the waste in the holds. The slave ships smelled so horrible that sailors on other ships often could tell that a slave ship was in the vicinity just by the odor, which carried on the ocean winds for long distances.

An Eyewitness On Board

Rev. Robert Walsh described the sight of slaves being released from the hold:

It is impossible to conceive the effect of this eruption—517 fellow creatures of all ages and sexes, some children, some adults, some old men and women, all in a state of total nudity, scrambling out together to taste the luxury of a little fresh air and water. They came swarming up like bees from the aperture of a hive till the whole deck was crowded to suffocation front stem to stern, so that it was impossible to imagine where they could all have come from or how they could have been stowed away.[3]

Escape and Death

Given the conditions aboard slave ships, coupled with a completely unknown future and the long voyage, many slaves felt that death was better than their situation. Some tried to jump over the sides of the ship when they were allowed on deck. Others tried to starve or poison themselves. But slaves were valuable cargo that the captain didn't want to lose. Some installed nets on ships to prevent slaves from jumping. Slaves who managed to make it into the water were often retrieved by crew members in small boats.

Slave traders also employed brutal ways to stop slaves from starving themselves to death. The first was punishment, which also served as an example to other slaves. Slaves who still refused to eat were often force-fed.

Sailors would force a special piece of equipment down the slave's throat and pour food down the device.

Some African captives tried to break free of the slave traders and rebel. Rebellion and mutiny could quickly spread, especially since many crew members were also mistreated and desperate. The captains used strong measures to stop any rebellious behavior and create an example for other slaves who might also try to rebel. Punishments included beatings, whippings, or the use of thumbscrews, torture devices that crushed the victim's thumbs. The captains believed they had to keep order at all costs. Therefore, many captains were harsh and violent. That attitude passed down through their chain of command. In 1884, the writer known as Dicky Sam, speaking about the slave trade around the turn of

SHARKS AND SLAVE SHIPS

Groups of hungry sharks followed slave ships. The Dutch merchant William Bosman wrote in his book *A New and Accurate Description of the Coast of Guinea*, published in the early 1700s:

> When dead Slaves are thrown over-board, I have sometimes, not without horrour, seen the dismal Rapaciousness of these Animals [sharks]; four or five of them together shoot to the bottom under the Ship to tear the dead Corps to pieces, at each bite an Arm, a Leg, or the Head is snapt off; and before you can tell twenty have sometimes divided the Body amongst them so nicely that not the least Particle is left.[4]

the 1800s, wrote, "The captain bullies the men, the men torture the slaves, the slaves' hearts are breaking with despair."[5]

THE SLAVE SHIP *ZONG*

Slave traders wanted their captives in the best possible condition in order to sell for a good price once they reached slave markets in the Caribbean or North America. However, because slaves were considered cargo, if any were lost by drowning, the ship's insurers compensated the owners for the loss. Insurance didn't pay for slaves lost due to illness. In 1781, this fact led to one of the most notorious incidents of cruelty in the Middle Passage.

The *Zong*, a slave ship heading to Jamaica from West Africa, had been at sea for 12 weeks with 417 slaves on board.[6] The ship was running out of water and illness had broken out among the captives. The captain decided that because the slaves would most likely

THE SLAVE SHIP IN ART

In 1840, artist J. M. W. Turner painted *Slave Ship (Slavers Throwing Overboard the Dead and Dying, Typhoon Coming On)*. It was exhibited in London at the Royal Academy. Turner was inspired by the story of the slave ship *Zong*, whose crew threw slaves overboard in order to claim insurance for their value. He was also influenced by the abolitionist movement in Britain. The painting brought public attention to slavery and helped further the abolitionist cause.

Sailors threw people off the *Zong* so they wouldn't lose money.

die anyway, he could reduce the financial loss to their owner by throwing the sick slaves overboard. That way, they would drown and the ship's owner would become eligible for insurance reimbursement. The captain ordered that 54 slaves be chained together and thrown overboard

to drown. Over the following two days, an additional
78 slaves were drowned.[7]

When the ship returned to England after leaving
its cargo in Jamaica, its owners filed a claim with the
insurance company for the value of the lost slaves. They
would probably have succeeded in getting compensation
if not for the former slave Olaudah Equiano, who was
now living in England. Equiano heard about the incident
and what had really happened to the slaves. He told his
abolitionist friend and the case went to court. The jury
members threw their support behind the owners. They
claimed that since it was permissible to slaughter animals
to keep the ship safe, it was okay to do the same to captive
people. However, the insurance company appealed the
decision. This time the court ruled that the slaves on board
the ship were people, not cargo. It was a landmark decision
for abolitionists seeking to assert the rights of slaves.

Between 1500 and 1866, 12.5 million enslaved Africans were forced to make the journey through the Middle Passage.[8] According to the estimates of some historians, millions died and were thrown into the Atlantic. Another 15 to 30 percent died when they were marched to or confined in slave castles.[9] The rest made it to the slave markets and were sold into lives of hard labor and often harsh treatment. And yet, despite the horrible conditions on the slave ships, some of the captives managed to rebel.

DISCUSSION STARTERS

- Is it important that people remember the history of the slave trade?

- In your opinion, what is the most horrific part of the slave trade?

- How do you think the world would be different today if the slave trade never existed?

THE SLAVE AUCTION

After being confined on board a slave ship for months, many slaves faced the horror of being sold at a public auction at their destination, either in the Caribbean or in the United States. When a slave ship was due to arrive in port, posters would be put up advertising that a slave auction would take place. It was at auctions that any families that had survived the voyage together usually would be broken up, as bidders might only want the strongest and healthiest slaves, or only men instead of women. When the ship arrived, the slaves were placed in a pen or enclosure. They were washed, and their skin was covered with grease or tar to make them look healthier and bring a higher price. If they hadn't been branded when they boarded the ship in Africa, they were branded at that time. Prospective buyers could then examine the slaves before the auction, poking them and looking at their teeth. Then the auction took place, with healthy male slaves priced highest, then women, and then children and the sick. The buyer with the highest bid purchased the slave.

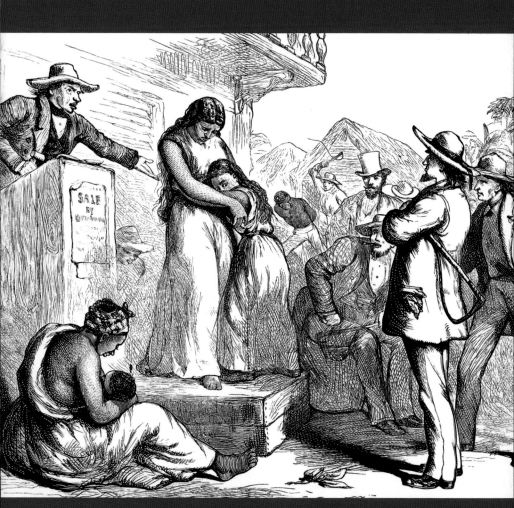

Enslaved people at slave auctions were assessed as though they were cattle.

THE *AMISTAD*

I n early 1839, Portuguese slave hunters in Sierra Leone caught and kidnapped a large group of Africans who were part of the Mende tribe. This was nothing unusual in itself, as the slave trade and the capture of free Africans had been taking place for hundreds of years. However, some of these captives would eventually lead a revolt on the *Amistad* ship.

The slave traders took their captives to the African coast. They were imprisoned in a slave depot called Lomboko, owned by a Spanish trader named Pedro Blanco. Blanco was rich and powerful. At Lomboko, captives were stripped, inspected, and held for several weeks. Some captives were then loaded onto the slave ship *Tecora* and sailed to Havana, Cuba, where they would be auctioned. Some of the captives later testified that on board

In 2007, an *Amistad* replica retraced Atlantic slave trade routes. The ship was built to honor the *Amistad* revolt.

the *Tecora,* they were shackled by the ankles, wrists, and neck. They were also forced to sleep in awkward positions in the hold without room to stand, and were often whipped for even minor offenses, such as not eating all of a meal. Every morning, the crew would bring up dead bodies from the lower deck and toss them overboard.

A Rebellion at Sea

At the Havana auction, two men from Spain—Don Pedro Montez and Don Jose Ruiz—bought 53 of the captives: four children and 49 adults.[1] This was technically an illegal action, because Cuba was a colony of Spain, and Spain had abolished slavery in its colonies in 1811. However, this law went largely unenforced. Ruiz and Montez loaded their captives onto a schooner called *Amistad*, which means "friendship" in Spanish. The schooner was traveling to the sugar plantations in Puerto Príncipe, Cuba, a few hundred miles from Havana. Ruiz and Montez left Havana at night to avoid being seen by British antislavery patrols. Thinking that the journey would take the usual four days, Ruiz and Montez stocked the ship with rations enough only for that time. They didn't expect that strong headwinds would slow their progress. Aboard the *Amistad*, the 53 captives continued to be mistreated. Sailors beat them and then poured salt, gunpowder, or rum into the fresh wounds to inflict maximum pain. The captives were also taunted by

Sengbe Pieh had a wife and three children at the time of his kidnapping.

the ship's cook, Celestino, who told them that they were
going to be killed, chopped up, and eaten by their captors.

However, just three days into the journey, the African
captives rebelled. They were led by a 25-year-old captive
and former rice farmer named Sengbe Pieh, whose name
had been changed by slave traders to Joseph Cinqué. His
name was changed to hide the fact that he was African,
as the slave traders were breaking the law. Even though
the captives came from nine different ethnic groups or
tribes, they communicated and agreed to band together

and fight back. They either broke or picked the locks on their shackles and freed themselves. Following Cinqué, the captives first climbed to the main deck, found Celestino, and bludgeoned him to death in his sleep. The other crew members awoke, but they didn't have time to load their guns before they were attacked. The captain used a dagger and a club to try to beat the captives off. He killed one African and wounded another before the captives slashed him to death, using knives for cutting sugarcane that they found in the ship's hold. Two crew members managed to throw a canoe overboard and escape in it.

The African captives tied up Montez and Ruiz and ordered them to sail the ship back to Africa. Because the captives had grown up away from the ocean, they had to rely on the two men to sail the ship and navigate a course. The Spaniards complied, sailing the ship to the east every day, using the sun to determine their course. However, unknown to Cinqué and his group, every night the men would secretly change the ship's course so it was heading north and west—away from Africa. They stopped at several islands in the Bahamas before moving north toward the US coast.

SEIZED

The *Amistad* sailed for two months. Soon there were reports of a mysterious black schooner, sailing erratically,

Death of Capt. Ferrer, the Captain of the Amistad, July, 1839.

Don Jose Ruiz and Don Pedro Montez, of the Island of Cuba, having purchased fifty-three slaves at Havana, recently imported from Africa, put them on board the Amistad, Capt. Ferrer, in order to transport them to Principe, another port on the Island of Cuba. After being out from Havana about four days, the African captives on board, in order to obtain their freedom, and return to Africa, armed themselves with cane knives, and rose upon the Captain and crew of the vessel. Capt. Ferrer and the cook of the vessel were killed; two of the crew escaped; Ruiz and Montez were made prisoners.

A newspaper printed its imaginings of the *Amistad* revolt.

with tattered sails and what appeared to be an all-black crew. The men aboard the *Amistad* were now suffering from extreme dehydration and dysentery because of a lack of fresh water on board, and several men died. In August 1839, the ship dropped its anchor just off Long Island, near New York City. The men planned to go ashore and get water and supplies.

The USS *Washington*, a US Navy ship, spotted the *Amistad*. Sailors boarded the ship and seized the nonhuman cargo, freed the two Spanish slave traders, and arrested the captives on board and those who had gone ashore. The African captives were put in a New Haven, Connecticut, prison. This was because slavery was illegal in New York but still legal in Connecticut. The Africans were charged with murder.

THE *CREOLE*

The *Amistad* wasn't the only slave-ship uprising. On October 27, 1841, a ship called the *Creole* left from Richmond, Virginia, carrying 135 captives to New Orleans, Louisiana.[2] This human trafficking occurred after the transatlantic slave trade was outlawed but while slave trading was still legal between US states. The slave trade between states still used ships to carry its human captives.

One of the slaves on board was Madison Washington, who had escaped slavery and traveled to Canada in 1840. He was captured and sold when he returned to Virginia hoping to find his wife, Susan. Washington didn't know that Susan was on the *Creole* with him, since men and women were kept separately. At least 14 slaves escaped from their shackles and made a surprise attack on the crew, killing some and capturing the rest, and arming themselves with the crew's muskets.[3] Washington, acting as captain, demanded that the ship be steered into British territory, where slavery was illegal. Only at this point did Susan and Washington realize they were on the same ship. The *Creole* eventually arrived in Nassau in the Bahamas, where British authorities set all the enslaved Africans free.

THE *AMISTAD* CASE GOES TO COURT

The Africans from the *Amistad* were kept in jail, but their story became a kind of media frenzy. Thousands of visitors paid to see them in their jail cells, and in New York City, theatergoers watched a play based on the *Amistad* incident, called *The Long, Low Black Schooner*. The *Amistad* conflict soon made its way into the federal courtroom in Hartford, Connecticut. Several cases were brought forth from the *Amistad* events, in addition to the murder charges against the Africans. The naval officers from the USS *Washington*, as well as two people who apprehended some of the Africans onshore, were suing for salvage rights. They claimed they should receive the value of the cargo, including the slaves. Ruiz and Montes were suing the US District Court for the return of their property. The Spanish and US governments were requesting that the Africans be returned to Cuba, even though it was almost certain that they would be executed

once they arrived. In addition, abolitionists wanted to use the case as an example of the evils of slavery.

At the Hartford trial, the judge ruled that the murder and conspiracy charges against the Africans should be dropped. But he also felt that the claims of the naval officers and the Spanish government were actually under the jurisdiction of a federal district court. The district

Cinqué's Testimony

Cinqué testified in court and described the rebellion. He said that the enslaved people on board the ship faced "great cruelty and oppression" by the crew and that they wanted to go home to their families in Africa. Cinqué noted that they took control of the ship "with the intent to return therein to their native country, or to seek an asylum in some free State where Slavery did not exist, in order that they might enjoy their liberty under the protection of its government."[4]

court judge then ruled that the Africans had been free men living in Africa and that the Spanish had no right to enslave them.

The judge ordered the Africans to be released and returned to Africa. But US President Martin Van Buren's administration immediately appealed the verdict, pressured by the Spanish government and worried about international diplomacy. They claimed that a treaty between Spain and the United States contained anti-piracy provisions and the Africans had acted as pirates.

The case went to the US Supreme Court in January 1841. Meanwhile, abolitionists had raised money for the Africans' defense and hired future Connecticut governor Roger Sherman Baldwin and former US president John Quincy Adams to defend them. Adams argued that Van Buren had abused his executive power when he tried to send the Africans back to Cuba. He waved a

A memorial for the *Amistad* is outside City Hall in New Haven.

FOONE

In August 1841, during the time when the freed *Amistad* captives were awaiting their return to Africa, one of them, a man named Foone, drowned in the Farmington River in Farmington, Connecticut. He was buried in Farmington's Riverside Cemetery with a tombstone marking his grave. Until 1992, it was the only Connecticut landmark honoring the *Amistad* and what many consider to be the country's first civil rights case.

copy of the Declaration of Independence in the courtroom, claiming that the case was a test of the United States' sincerity about its beliefs as written in the Declaration. He also defended the rights of the Africans to fight to regain their freedom. His passionate defense paid off, and the court agreed with him. On March 9, 1841, Senior Justice Joseph Story wrote in the decision: "it was the ultimate right of all human beings in extreme cases to resist oppression, and to apply force against ruinous injustice."[5] The Africans were declared free.

RETURNING HOME

Abolitionist groups raised the money needed to return the *Amistad* captives to Sierra Leone. There were only 35 survivors.[6] On November 26, 1841, the Africans, along with Christian missionaries, boarded a ship for Africa. They arrived in Sierra Leone seven weeks later. While some of the *Amistad* captives stayed with the missionaries, including a few children who took English names, the rest returned to their homes.

The *Amistad* was an important event in the transatlantic slave trade and to slavery in the United States. That's because Cinqué and the other captives were freed through court proceedings with the help of abolitionists. It was the first and only time that Africans who had been seized and brought to the country to become slaves won their freedom. The event created a legal basis for abolishing slavery itself.

DISCUSSION STARTERS

- Why do you think some slaves rebelled while on slave ships and others didn't?

- Why do you think the US president was more concerned with maintaining international diplomacy with Spain than freeing the captive people on the *Amistad*?

- Why do you think it's important to know about events such as the *Amistad* case?

CHAPTER SEVEN

ENDING THE TRADE

The transatlantic slave trade existed for 400 years, creating great wealth for the traders, merchants, and slaveholders involved. The trade carried millions of enslaved Africans to the Caribbean and the Americas and provided cheap slave-produced goods for consumers in the United States and Europe. But by the 1800s, many countries were starting to have second thoughts about trading humans, and many enslaved peoples were rebelling.

THE HAITIAN REVOLUTION

By the 1700s, Saint-Domingue in the Caribbean was one of France's wealthiest colonies. It produced sugar, coffee, indigo, and cotton. Most of these crops were produced by enslaved Africans who

Some art showing the Haitian Revolution evokes biased views of brutal black men hurting seemingly innocent white people.

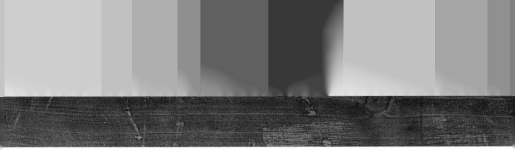

came to the colony through the slave trade. The slaves on Saint-Domingue were known for being rebellious. More than 500,000 black people lived there.[1] They consisted of three distinct groups: slaves, free blacks, and runaway slaves, who were known as maroons. The maroons lived in the mountains and farmed to survive. With a population ratio of ten blacks to each white person, colonial officials and plantation owners struggled to control them.

In 1791, a former slave named Toussaint Louverture led the slaves, and eventually other black people, in a rebellion against the white planters and the French colonial government. After fierce battling with French and then British forces, the rebels controlled the island by 1803. Louverture was arrested during the rebellion and sent to France, where he died, but his general Jean-Jacques Dessalines, also a former slave, carried on the battle. On January 1, 1804, Dessalines declared Saint-Domingue an independent nation and named it Haiti. Haiti was the first black republic in the world and the second nation in the Western Hemisphere, after the United States, to win independence from the European country that colonized it.

Congress Acts

When the United States was writing its Constitution, the question of whether to ban slavery or the slave

Toussaint Louverture was known as an effective military commander.

An Early Slave Rebellion

The Haitian Revolution was by no means the first slave rebellion. In 1570, an African slave named Gaspar Yanga staged a revolt against his slaveholders on a sugarcane plantation near Veracruz, Mexico, which was under Spanish control. Yanga and a group of slaves escaped from the plantation and fled into the forest. There they eventually established their own colony, San Lorenzo de los Negros. Yanga and his group managed to evade capture for 40 years, surviving by farming and by occasional raids on Spanish supply ships. The colony was destroyed in 1609, but the Spanish authorities were unable to capture Yanga. They eventually signed a peace treaty with him and his followers. In 1630, Yanga won the right to establish his own colony, as long as he paid taxes to the Spanish crown. This colony, which was the first official settlement of freed Africans in the Americas, still exists today as a town called Yanga.

trade was a source of conflict. Northern states had a growing opposition to slavery as a moral issue, whereas Southern states wanted to continue the system for economic reasons.

Importing slaves had been banned during the American Revolution (1775–1783), but as the Constitution was being written, Southern states expected the slave trade to open again. They wanted slaves to work in the South. The result of this conflict was the provision in Article 1, Section 9 of the Constitution, written in 1787, which prevented Congress from ending the slave trade before 1808. The South fully expected that by 1808, its states would have enough political power to keep Congress from permanently ending the slave trade.

Although Congress couldn't end the slave trade until 1808, it did take steps to regulate it. In the Act of 1794, Congress prohibited any US shipyard or port from building or equipping any vessel to be used in the slave trade. Any ships sailing from US ports were prohibited from engaging in slave trafficking as well—even if they were registered in a foreign country. Penalties for breaking this law included fines ranging from $2,000 for outfitting a ship to $200 for a person working on a slave ship.[2] In addition, anyone who informed on a ship breaking this law was entitled to half of the fines, making it lucrative for ship's captains to inform on each other.

But in 1800, Georgia and South Carolina made the slave trade legal again in their states, opening up international slave trading once more and bringing 100,000 Africans into the United States as slaves within eight years.[3] As a result, Congress amended its 1794 act with the Act of 1800, which made it illegal to invest in the transatlantic slave trade, even if the slaves were transported legally by non-US ships. In addition, it was now illegal for any US citizen to work on a slave ship. And because slavery was legal in some US states and illegal in others, Congress also added the Act of 1803. This act

Although the United States looked for ways to regulate the slave trade in the late 1700s, slavery itself would continue for decades.

levied new fines for people who brought newly arrived slaves, whether from Africa or the Caribbean, into states where the international slave trade was illegal. Finally, Congress passed legislation banning all importation of slaves as of January 1, 1808. The United States was legally out of the transatlantic slave trade. In 1820, the United States also declared that slave trading was an act of piracy and was punishable by the death penalty.

Britain Steps Up

Britain was one of the principal participants in the international slave trade. Its ports benefited from the money transatlantic trade shipping generated, and its citizens benefited from the cheap, plentiful goods it produced. But many British people opposed slavery on moral grounds. Between 1780 and 1830, petitions were gathered with hundreds of thousands of signatures of people who wanted slavery to end. Abolitionists helped spread awareness of the evils of slavery, too. Finally, in 1807, Britain passed laws to abolish its involvement in the international slave trade. In 1833 it banned the use of slaves in any British territory.

The British also negotiated several treaties with Spain and Portugal aimed at abolishing the slave trade. At the 1815 Congress of Vienna, it pressured Spain, Portugal, France, and the Netherlands to agree to abolish the slave

Nathaniel Gordon and the Slave Trade

Captain Nathaniel Gordon was the only American ship captain to be arrested, convicted, and executed for slave trading under the Act of 1820. Gordon had been a pirate along the US coast before he began slave trading. On August 7, 1860, he loaded 897 slaves on his ship in Africa.[4] The very next day, he was intercepted by the USS *Mohican* and arrested. The slaves were taken to Liberia. In 1861, he was tried and convicted in a federal court in New York and sentenced to death by hanging.

trade. However, with the economies of Cuba and Brazil expanding because of their slave trading, the goal of a complete worldwide ban on slave trading was still elusive.

STOPPING THE TRADE

After 1807, Britain tried to create a network of treaties to regulate the slave trade. However, many countries weren't included in these treaties. Slave ships could fly the flags of countries such as Mexico, Russia, Sardinia, and Argentina and be safe from British patrols and interference. In addition, Brazil and Cuba continued to trade in slaves and welcomed slave-trading ships to their ports.

Slave-trading ships also often hid under false US flags, knowing that the US flag would most likely prevent British patrol ships from stopping and searching them. But that changed in 1862. That's because some Southern states had seceded from the country, forming the Confederate States of America. That year, the United States signed a treaty with Britain that allowed both countries to stop and search each other's ships freely if slave trading was suspected. Slave trading began to decrease.

Although the United States banned international slave trading in 1807 and agreed to help police the seas, the country only ever assigned six of its warships to patrol duty.[5] And in some years, there weren't any US patrol ships. Until the beginning of the US Civil War

Millions of African captives were taken across the Red Sea to Asia between 1500 and 1900. Some European patrol ships stopped them.

(1861–1865), Britain was responsible for detaining 80 percent of the ships that were stopped and charged with transporting slaves.[6] The reason the United States was hesitant to participate was that many Southern leaders opposed serious action on slave trading because the South's economy heavily relied on slave labor. In addition, American-built yachts and clipper ships, which found their way into the hands of slave traders, were so fast that they reduced the time it took to travel the Middle Passage to Cuba. Some slave ships sailing after 1810 were built in

An artist imagines a celebration in the House of Representatives after the Thirteenth Amendment is enacted.

US ports—despite the fact that US participation in the trade was illegal—a contribution to the US economy that shipbuilders were reluctant to lose. However, the Civil War led to the abolishment of slavery in the United States with the Thirteenth Amendment to the Constitution in 1865.

Slavery continued in North Africa, the Middle East, and the Indian Ocean. It still existed in sub-Saharan Africa during the early 1900s. Slavery occurs today, with an estimated 45 million people worldwide still enslaved in some form.[7] While it's illegal under the traditional definition of slavery—where a person is treated as legal property—the modern definition of slavery is a situation from which a person can't escape because of threats of violence, abuse of power, deception, or coercion. Forms of modern slavery include human trafficking, forced marriages, forced labor, and the sale and exploitation of children.

DISCUSSION STARTERS

- Why do you think some countries wanted to ban the slave trade and others didn't?

- Why do you think Britain pushed other countries to abolish the slave trade?

- Why do you think some people valued economic prosperity more than human rights?

LEGACY

The transatlantic slave trade ended, but it left a legacy that's still evident today. Slavery and the slave trade played a huge role in the economic development of countries such as Britain. The Industrial Revolution occurred there in the late 1700s to early 1800s. During that time, machinery was introduced into manufacturing and farming. This revolution benefited from slavery's role in the US production of raw cotton, which supported the textile mills that blossomed during this period. Even after Britain outlawed slavery, it still received payback from its investments in the slave trade and the slavery occurring in the United States, Cuba, and Brazil.

The transatlantic slave trade also fueled the growth of US capitalism. New England textile

Today, some US institutions connected with the slave trade acknowledge their past. One example is Brown University, which benefited from the trade and now has a memorial.

mills depended on Southern cotton, which was produced through slave labor. Banks and insurance companies made money from the slave trade and from insuring slaves as property. Distilleries that made rum from sugar and molasses sold the rum to companies that in turn sold it to finance the purchase of more slaves. Shipbuilders profited by building and selling faster ships for use in the slave trade. Outfitters made money from supplying the fittings and the supplies for slave ships. This commerce had public benefits as well, since families that made a great deal of money from slavery often used that money to endow schools, colleges, and libraries.

THE SCRAMBLE FOR AFRICA

Because of their involvement in the slave trade and their increased familiarity with Africa, major European powers such as Britain continued their presence on the continent even after the slave trade ended. By the end of the 1800s, many European powers were involved in what was called the scramble for Africa. The European nations invaded the continent and began colonizing it. As explorers followed in the footsteps of slave traders and reached the interior of Africa, they found riches such as ivory, gold, diamonds, emeralds, and copper. They also realized that they could set up plantations to produce crops, such as cotton and palm oil, with cheap African labor instead of buying these

Britain still had a presence in West Africa into the mid-1900s.

commodities from villagers or other sources. Eventually, countries such as Britain, Germany, and Belgium met and divided the continent between themselves. The European countries easily crushed any resistance to their colonization. They treated Africans as if they were children who couldn't take care of themselves.

Meanwhile, all profits from Africa's natural resources, such as minerals and good farmland, went to Europe. Europeans exploited so much of Africa's potential industry and economy that Africans had little ability to create and manage economies of their own.

Under colonial rule, the European quest to make money resulted in the planting and harvesting of just one or two crops that were specifically planted to meet the needs of European markets. Unlike a more diverse agriculture, with crops suited to the climate and the needs of the African people, growing only a few crops for commercial purposes might mean that those crops were not well suited to Africa, did not feed Africans, and were vulnerable to droughts or other climate events. If those crops failed, agriculture as a whole failed.

Africans were also unable to establish their own banks, factories, and shipping companies. Most of the institutions that operated there were part of European companies. As European economies developed and flourished, African economies became increasingly underdeveloped.

From the 1500s through the mid-1900s, Africa also lost millions of people—a huge blow to its population. This wasn't just due to the numbers of Africans who were enslaved and sent

THE EXCEPTIONS

Two African countries avoided European colonization in the 1800s. Liberia, located in West Africa, was established by abolitionists in the United States as a place for freed African slaves and their descendants. It became an independent state in 1847, and by 1867 thousands of freed slaves had moved there. Ethiopia managed to remain independent during the scramble for Africa by successfully defeating Italy's takeover attempts in 1896, which prevented other European colonizers from trying the same thing. Ethiopia retained its independence until just before World War II (1939–1945), when it went through a period of Italian control from 1936 to 1941. In 1941, the Italians were pushed out in part by Ethiopian and British forces.

to other countries during the transatlantic trade. Colonial rule often also resulted in the loss of many African lives, with millions dying in the conflicts between colonizers and African kingdoms.

A Legacy of Racism

Even after the slave trade and slavery ended, Africans suffered from racism. Under colonial rule, they faced discrimination under law and were considered inferior and incapable of governing themselves. This led to the system of apartheid in Africa, which was introduced in South Africa in 1948. Apartheid was legislated discrimination by race, and it existed in South Africa until 1991.

In the United States, the period following the Civil War and Thirteenth Amendment didn't give African Americans equality with white people. White supremacist organizations such as the Ku Klux Klan (KKK) grew in strength. In the South, anyone of African origin was discriminated against and segregated by Jim Crow laws.

African Persecution

In the Kiswahili language, spoken by the Swahili people of Africa, the word *Maafa* means disaster, great tragedy, or terrible occurrence. It describes what happened to their people during the transatlantic slave trade. Specifically, it refers to 500 years of suffering by African peoples, including slavery, imperialism, colonialism, apartheid, rape, oppression, invasions, and exploitation.

BLACK CODES

In the US South following the Civil War, Black Codes were enacted to control what African Americans could do. Blacks were forced to sign annual labor contracts—written proof that they would have employment the next year—or risk paying a fine or being forced into unpaid labor. In South Carolina, blacks were forced to pay an annual tax of $10 to $100 if they performed any other occupation than that of farmer or servant.[2] The codes restricted the freedom of African Americans in both work and other activities, and lasted until the end of Reconstruction in 1877. However, they essentially continued under the guise of the Jim Crow laws.

These laws, like apartheid in Africa, legalized a system where it was permissible and acceptable to discriminate against African Americans. The laws forced African Americans to have separate and often inferior schools compared to white people, as well as separate sections of restaurants, drinking fountains, buses, trains, parks, and libraries. Supposedly this segregation was based on separate but equal treatment, but the facilities were rarely equivalent in quality. Moreover, as civil rights activist Diane Nash said in 2017, speaking of these laws, "The very fact that there were separate facilities was to say to black people and white people that blacks were so subhuman and so inferior that we could not even use the public facilities that white people used."[1]

Segregation laws were enforced by local police.

In addition, most blacks in the South were barred from voting. State governments in the South forced people to take biased literacy tests before being allowed to vote. These tests were meant to exclude many African Americans.

Jim Crow laws lasted until the Civil Rights Act of 1964 outlawed them. The civil rights movement of the 1950s and 1960s, when African Americans fought for freedoms such as voting rights, desegregation, and equal housing and employment opportunities, brought issues of inequality into focus and resulted in many changes, especially in the South.

However, the descendants of the Africans who were enslaved and forced to travel the Middle Passage to the United States are still dealing with the legacy of racism and inequality every day. For example, the Black Lives Matter campaign, which began in 2013 in response to police killings of black people, struggles against violence and racism still aimed at African Americans. Activists take on issues such as racial profiling, police brutality, and racial inequality in the criminal justice system. In some ways, the struggles of the civil rights movement are still evident in the daily lives of African Americans, no matter how many generations they are removed from the slave trade era.

A LEGACY OF THEIR OWN

The Africans who came to the United States through the Middle Passage brought with them their folklore, language, music, and food. African folktales created the stories of Uncle Remus and Brer Rabbit in the South, the Anansi tales in Jamaica, and the Bouki trickster tales in Haiti. These tales, which are common in mythology and folklore, usually feature a main character who might be physically weak but uses cleverness to deceive a larger, stronger opponent. New languages such as Creole that combined African, European, and American languages emerged. Call-and-response singing and gospel music based on African musical traditions developed new forms of American music, influencing rock and roll, jazz, blues, and hip-hop. Even everyday rituals such as cooking, eating, and dressing affected US culture, as Africans blended their culture with that of the United States.

In 2015, the United Nations (UN) erected a memorial to the victims of the transatlantic slave trade. Located at the UN headquarters in New York City, the memorial is called the Ark of Return. It's dedicated to the enslaved peoples, abolitionists, and others who helped to end slavery, as well as the continuing contributions of Africans and their descendants in the United States. It

People can visit the Ark of Return memorial to gain a greater understanding of the slave trade.

consists of three sections: "Acknowledge the tragedy," a three-dimensional map of Africa and the slave trade; "Consider the legacy," a life-size human figure carved from Zimbabwe black granite and occupying a space of the same dimensions most slaves had on slave ships; and "Lest we forget," a large reflecting pool for visitors to view and think about the millions of lives lost.[4] Rodney Leon, a US architect of Haitian descent, designed the memorial. It was dedicated March 25, 2015, on the UN's International Day of Remembrance of the Victims of Slavery and the Transatlantic Slave Trade.

At the dedication, UN Secretary-General Ban Ki-moon said, "This poignant and powerful memorial helps us to acknowledge the collective tragedy that befell millions of people. It encourages us to consider the historical legacy of slavery and above all, it ensures that we never forget."[5] By remembering the millions of Africans who were captured and enslaved or who died in the process, it's hoped that the world will never again repeat a tragedy of this scale.

DISCUSSION STARTERS

- Have you seen or experienced racism? What can an individual do to help stop racism?

- How did the legacy of slavery lead to the civil rights movement of the 1950s and 1960s?

- Do you think that slavery will ever be completely eliminated in the world? Why or why not?

1300s
The Portuguese begin to explore the coast of Africa.

1444
Portuguese traders arrive on the coast of Africa.

1490s
Sugarcane plantations are built on the island of São Tomé off the coast of Africa.

1518
The first shipment of slaves sails from Africa to the Americas.

1600s
Britain enters the transatlantic slave trade.

1685
King Louis XIV of France establishes the Code Noir.

1735
A six-year-old African prince named Venture Smith is captured and then sold to slave traders.

1781
The captain of the slave ship *Zong* throws 132 slaves overboard and then claims them as an insurance loss.

1789
Olaudah Equiano publishes his book *The Interesting Narrative of the Life of Olaudah Equiano or Gustavus Vassa, the African*.

1791
Toussaint Louverture leads the slave rebellion in Saint-Domingue.

1807
Britain passes a law making it illegal to buy, sell, or transport slaves.

1808
The United States abolishes the slave trade.

1811
Spain abolishes slavery in its colonies.

1829
Rev. Walsh boards a slave ship and records the inhuman conditions found there.

1839
The *Amistad* slave ship rebellion takes place.

1841
The *Amistad* case goes to the Supreme Court; the captured Africans are freed.

1861–1865
The US Civil War takes place.

1865
The Thirteenth Amendment to the Constitution abolishes slavery in the United States.

SIGNIFICANT EVENTS

- The first Portuguese slave traders arrived in Africa in the 1400s. They began to capture and enslave Africans.

- In 1518, captive Africans were shipped from Africa to the Americas by Spanish slave traders.

- Throughout the 1700s, the transatlantic slave trade continued and became more and more sophisticated.

- In 1807, the British made slave trading illegal. Other countries followed their example within the next decade.

- The United States banned the importation of slaves in 1808.

KEY PLAYERS

- European slave traders kidnapped millions of Africans and forced them into slavery.

- The United States participated in slavery to further its economic advancement.

- Olaudah Equiano was kidnapped, enslaved, and eventually freed. He wrote a groundbreaking book about his experience.

- The group of African captives on the *Amistad* was declared free by the Supreme Court. This was an important moment in the fight to abolish slavery.

IMPACT ON SOCIETY

Millions of Africans were forced to leave their homeland and become slaves. They faced horrific conditions on slave ships. If they survived the journey across the Atlantic Ocean, they endured a lifetime of labor as slaves. The legacy of the transatlantic slave trade continued long after it was outlawed. It planted seeds of racism that took root in the United States, and the country still struggles with racism toward black people today.

QUOTE

"Is it not enough that we are torn from our country and friends to toil for your luxury and lust of gain? . . . Why are parents to lose their children, brothers their sisters, or husbands their wives? Surely this is a new refinement in cruelty, which . . . aggravates distress, and adds fresh horrors even to the wretchedness of slavery."

—*Olaudah Equiano*

abolitionist
Someone who works to put an end to slavery.

bilateral
Involving two sides.

capitalism
An economic system in which businesses are privately owned and operated for the purpose of making a profit.

commodity
Something that has value and is bought and sold.

compensate
To give someone money to make up for lost or damaged property.

diplomacy
The skill of maintaining relationships between governments.

dysentery
A bacterial disease that causes severe diarrhea.

piracy
The action of attacking and robbing ships at sea.

plantation
A large farm or estate where crops such as cotton, sugar, and tobacco are grown, usually by laborers who live on the estate.

racism
Inferior treatment of a person or group of people based on race.

schooner
A ship that has at least two masts.

secede
To formally withdraw from a political union.

segregation
The practice of separating groups of people based on race, gender, ethnicity, or other factors.

trafficking
Dealing or trading in something.

treaty
An agreement between two or more countries or leaders.

ADDITIONAL RESOURCES

SELECTED BIBLIOGRAPHY

Adi, Hakim. "Africa and the Transatlantic Slave Trade." *BBC*, 5 Oct. 2012, bbc.co.uk. Accessed 8 Oct. 2018.

Equiano, Olaudah. *The Interesting Narrative of the Life of Olaudah Equiano, Or Gustavus Vassa, The African*. W. Durell, 1791.

"The Journey: The Middle Passage." *BBC*, n.d., bbc.co.uk. Accessed 8 Oct. 2018.

FURTHER READINGS

Bakshi, Kelly. *Roots of Racism*. Abdo, 2018.

Harris, Duchess. *How Slaves Built America*. Abdo, 2020.

ONLINE RESOURCES

To learn more about the transatlantic slave trade, please visit **abdobooklinks.com** or scan this QR code. These links are routinely monitored and updated to provide the most current information available.

MORE INFORMATION

For more information on this subject, contact or visit the following organizations:

NATIONAL MUSEUM OF AFRICAN AMERICAN HISTORY & CULTURE

1400 Constitution Ave. NW
Washington, DC, 20560
844-750-3012
nmaahc.si.edu
The National Museum of African American History & Culture opened in 2016. This museum has tens of thousands of artifacts illuminating African American history and culture. There are also exhibits on the history of slavery.

UNITED NATIONS EDUCATIONAL, SCIENTIFIC AND CULTURAL ORGANIZATION (UNESCO)

2 United Nations Plaza
New York, NY 10017
1-917-810-9030
unesco.org
UNESCO has many resources on slavery and the slave trade.

SOURCE NOTES

CHAPTER 1. SHIP OF GRIEF

1. "Aboard a Slave Ship, 1829." *Eyewitness to History*, n.d., eyewitnesstohistory.com. Accessed 28 Dec. 2018.

2. "Aboard a Slave Ship, 1829."

3. David Dabydeen. "Poetic License." *Guardian*, 2 Dec. 2005, theguardian.com. Accessed 28 Dec. 2018.

4. Olaudah Equiano. *The Interesting Narrative of the Life of Olaudah Equiano, or Gustavus Vassa, The African. Written by Himself.* Project Gutenberg, 2005.

5. "The Journey: The Middle Passage." *BBC*, n.d., bbc.co.uk. Accessed 28 Dec. 2018.

6. "Equiano's Autobiography." *PBS*, n.d., pbs.org. Accessed 28 Dec. 2018.

7. "Mending an Era: A Slave Ship Speaks." *Department of West Virginia Arts, Culture and History*, n.d., wvculture.org. Accessed 28 Dec. 2018.

8. "The Journey."

9. Equiano, *The Interesting Narrative of the Life of Olaudah Equiano*.

CHAPTER 2. AFRICA BEFORE THE SLAVE TRADE

1. "West Africa before the Europeans." *National Archives*, n.d., nationalarchives.gov.uk. Accessed 28 Dec. 2018.

2. "The Narrative of Louis Asa-Asa & the Transatlantic Slave Trade." *Mary Prince*, n.d., maryprince.org. Accessed 28 Dec. 2018.

CHAPTER 3. EUROPE STEPS IN

1. Ole Benedictow. "The Black Death: The Greatest Catastrophe Ever." *History Today*, 3 Mar. 2005, historytoday.com. Accessed 28 Dec. 2018.

2. "The Portuguese in Africa, 1415–1600." *Met Museum*, Oct. 2002, metmuseum.org. Accessed 28 Dec. 2018.

3. Dr. Hakim Adi. "Africa and the Transatlantic Slave Trade." *Academia*, 17 Feb. 2011, academia.edu. Accessed 28 Dec. 2018.

4. "Iberian Slave Trade." *Slavery and Remembrance*, n.d., slaveryandremembrance.org. Accessed 28 Dec. 2018.

5. "Dutch Slave Trade." *Slavery and Remembrance*, n.d., slaveryandremembrance.org. Accessed 28 Dec. 2018.

6. "Dutch Slave Trade."

7. "British Slave Trade." *Slavery and Remembrance*, n.d., slaveryandremembrance.org. Accessed 28 Dec. 2018.

8. "French Slave Trade." *Slavery and Remembrance*, n.d., slaveryandremembrance.org. Accessed 28 Dec. 2018.

9. Nicole Atwill. "Slavery in the French Colonies: Le Code Noir (the Black Code) of 1685." *Library of Congress*, 13 Jan. 2011, blogs.loc.gov. Accessed 28 Dec. 2018.

CHAPTER 4. TRANSATLANTIC TRADING

1. "The Story of . . . Smallpox—and Other Deadly Eurasian Germs." *PBS*, n.d., pbs.org. Accessed 28 Dec. 2018.

2. "Transatlantic Slave Trade Was Not Entirely 'Triangular'—Countries in the Americas Sent Ships Out Too." *Conversation*, 23 Aug. 2018, theconversation.com. Accessed 28 Dec. 2018.

3. "Transatlantic Slave Trade Was Not Entirely 'Triangular.'"

4. "Former Slave Venture Smith Tells the Story of His Capture in Africa at Age 6." *New England Historical Society*, n.d., newenglandhistoricalsociety.com. Accessed 28 Dec. 2018.

5. "Capture: Selections from the Narratives of Former Slaves." *National Humanities Center*, n.d., nationalhumanitiescenter.org. Accessed 28 Dec. 2018.

6. "Capture."

7. "The Slave Route." *UNESCO*, n.d., unesco.org. Accessed 28 Dec. 2018.

CHAPTER 5. THE MIDDLE PASSAGE

1. "The Middle Passage." *Digital History*, n.d., digitalhistory.uh.edu. Accessed 28 Dec. 2018.

2. Brendan Wolfe. "Slave Ships and the Middle Passage." *Encyclopedia Virginia*, 17 Apr. 2012, encyclopediavirginia.org. Accessed 28 Dec. 2018.

3. "Aboard a Slave Ship, 1829." *Eyewitness to History*, n.d., eyewitnesstohistory.com. Accessed 28 Dec. 2018.

4. Wolfe, "Slave Ships and the Middle Passage."

5. Wolfe, "Slave Ships and the Middle Passage."

6. "Living Africans Thrown Overboard." *PBS*, n.d., pbs.org. Accessed 28 Dec. 2018.

7. "Living Africans Thrown Overboard."

8. Wolfe, "Slave Ships and the Middle Passage."

9. "The Middle Passage."

CHAPTER 6. THE *AMISTAD*

1. Jesse Greenspan. "The *Amistad* Slave Rebellion, 175 Years Ago." *History*, 2 July 2014, history.com. Accessed 28 Dec. 2018.

2. "5 Slave Ship Uprisings Other Than *Amistad*." *Atlanta Black Star*, 7 Feb. 2015, atlantablackstar.com. Accessed 28 Dec. 2018.

3. "5 Slave Ship Uprisings Other Than *Amistad*."

4. "Plea to the Jurisdiction of Cinque and Others." *Docs Teach*, 21 Aug. 1839, docsteach.org. Accessed 28 Dec. 2018.

5. "Trafficking in Humans." *National Archives*, n.d., archives.gov. Accessed 28 Dec. 2018.

6. Greenspan, "The *Amistad* Slave Rebellion."

CHAPTER 7. ENDING THE TRADE

1. "Haitian Revolution (1791–1804)." *Black Past*, n.d., blackpast.org. Accessed 28 Dec. 2018.

2. "Regulating the Trade." *Schomburg Center for Research in Black Culture*, n.d., abolition.nypl.org. Accessed 28 Dec. 2018.

3. "Regulating the Trade."

4. Michael Coard. "America's Only Execution of a Slave Trader." *Philadelphia Tribune*, 18 Feb. 2017, phillytrib.com. Accessed 28 Dec. 2018.

5. David Eltis and David Richardson. "The Transatlantic Slave Trade and the Civil War." *New York Times*, 13 Jan. 2011, nytimes.com. Accessed 28 Dec. 2018.

6. Eltis and Richardson, "The Transatlantic Slave Trade and the Civil War."

7. Eltis and Richardson, "The Transatlantic Slave Trade and the Civil War."

CHAPTER 8. LEGACY

1. "Jim Crow Laws." *PBS*, n.d., pbs.org. Accessed 28 Dec. 2018.

2. "Black Codes." *History*, n.d., history.com. Accessed 28 Dec. 2018.

3. "World Yet to Overcome Racism as Slavery's Legacy 'Resounds down the Ages,' Secretary-General Tells Tribute Event for Victims of Transatlantic Trade." *United Nations*, 24 Mar. 2017, un.org. Accessed 28 Dec. 2018.

4. "The Ark of Return." *UNESCO*, n.d., unesco.org. Accessed 28 Dec. 2018.

5. Jacqueline Charles. "United Nations Unveils Slavery Memorial." *Miami Herald*, 25 Mar. 2015, miamiherald.com. Accessed 28 Dec. 2018.

DUCHESS HARRIS, JD, PHD

Dr. Harris is a professor of American Studies at Macalester College and curator of the Duchess Harris Collection of ABDO books. She is also the coauthor of the titles in the collection, which features popular selections such as *Hidden Human Computers: The Black Women of NASA* and series including News Literacy and Being Female in America.

Before working with ABDO, Dr. Harris authored several other books on the topics of race, culture, and American history. She served as an associate editor for *Litigation News*, the American Bar Association Section of Litigation's quarterly flagship publication, and was the first editor in chief of *Law Raza*, an interactive online journal covering race and the law, published at William Mitchell College of Law. She has earned a PhD in American Studies from the University of Minnesota and a JD from William Mitchell College of Law.

MARCIA AMIDON LUSTED

Marcia Amidon Lusted has written 160 books and 600 magazine articles for young readers. She is also the former editor of *AppleSeeds* magazine for children. You can find out more about her books at www.adventuresinnonfiction.com.